My Neighbors and Their

Simple Machines

TeachingStrategies® • Bethesda, MD

Copyright © 2016 by Teaching Strategies, LLC

All rights reserved. No part of this publication may be reproduced in any form or by any electronic or mechanical means, including information storage and retrieval systems, without the prior written permission of Teaching Strategies, LLC.

The publisher and the authors cannot be held responsible for injury, mishap, or damages incurred during the use of or because of this information in this book. The authors recommend appropriate and reasonable supervision at all times based on the age and capability of each child.

Design and layout: Propellor-id.com

Teaching Strategies, LLC
Bethesda, Maryland
TeachingStrategies.com

978-1-60617-727-3

Teaching Strategies name and logo are registered trademarks of Teaching Strategies, LLC, Bethesda, MD.

CPSIA tracking label information:
RR Donnelley, Dongguan, China
Date of Production: December 2020
Cohort: Batch 1

Printed and bound in China

2 3 4 5 6 7 8 9
Printing

24 23 22 21 20
Year Printed

Hi! My name is Ama, and I live in an apartment building in the city. I love living in my building because I get to visit my interesting neighbors.

Let's see what they are doing today!

That's Mr. Salgado, who is here to clean the windows on the outside of our building. He uses a seat on a rope to reach them. Mr. Salgado uses a **PULLEY** to raise and lower his seat.

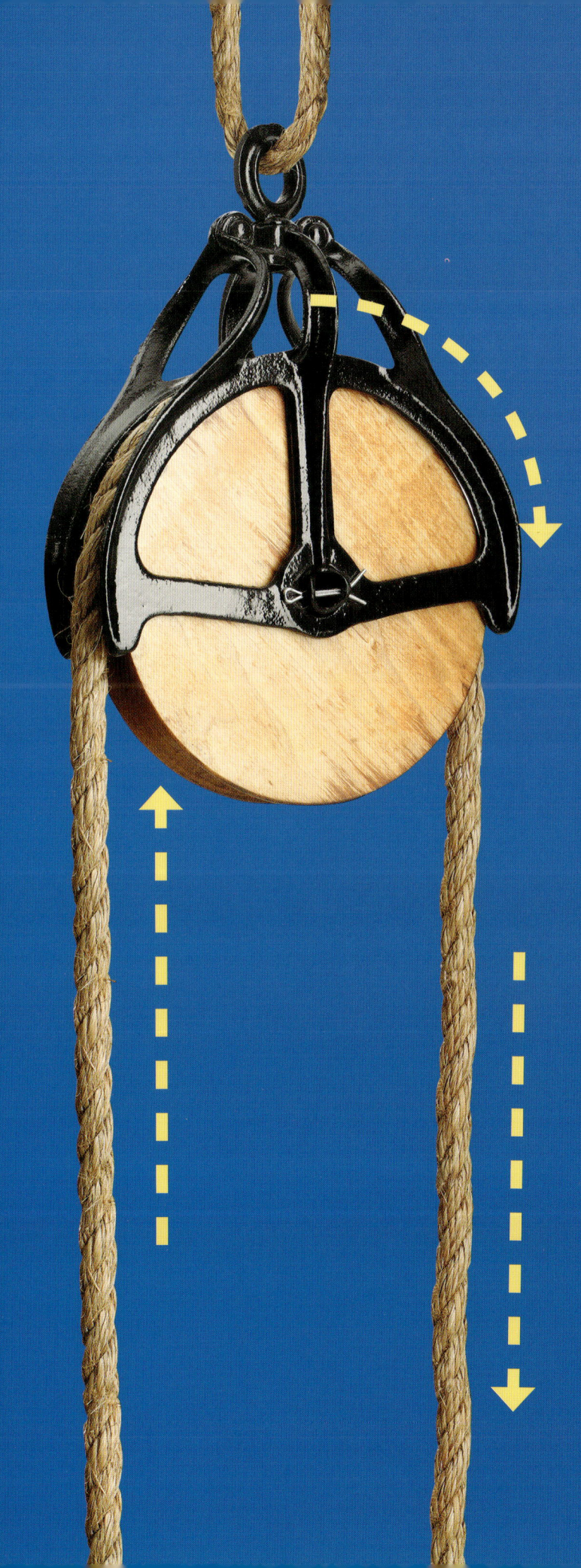

pulley

A **PULLEY** is a type of simple machine that uses a rope and a small wheel to help raise and lower things. The pulley helps Mr. Salgado move up and down the outside of the building. Pulling down on the rope makes it easier to lift something heavy.

Sometimes **PULLEYS** have more than one wheel. The more wheels a pulley has, the easier it is to lift things.

Mmm, I smell something good baking down the hall. Mrs. D'Angelo is baking fresh bread again. I stop by her apartment, and she offers me a big slice. Yum! Mrs. D'Angelo uses a knife to slice the fresh bread that she baked.

wedge

A knife is a **WEDGE**, which is a type of simple machine that splits things apart.

WEDGES are shaped like triangles. Wedges can be big like an axe, or they can be small like the tip of a nail. Teeth, doorstops, and forks are also examples of wedges.

My mom and I are visiting with our neighbor Mrs. Howard and her son Tredell. Tredell and I want to play with his toy cars, but the **WHEEL** and **AXLE** broke on one of them.

6

A **WHEEL** and **AXLE** is a type of simple machine that helps move things like cars, wagons, and wheelbarrows.

Wheel

Axle

The **AXLE** goes through the middle of the **WHEEL**, and the wheel and axle turn together to move things. A wheelbarrow has one wheel and axle. A tractor trailer can have as many as nine axles and eighteen wheels.

Instead of playing with toy cars, Tredell and I decide to make paper snowflakes out of colorful paper. We first fold the paper and then use scissors to cut out small shapes.

Scissors are a type of **LEVER**, which is a simple machine.

lever

A **LEVER** is a rod or a bar that pivots at a point called the fulcrum. The fulcrum can be in the middle of the lever or at the end of the lever. Scissors are made of two levers with a fulcrum that joins them together in the middle.

Later on, I meet my friend Jack down at the playground behind our apartment building. My favorite thing at the playground is the seesaw. Jack loves it, too!

lever

The ends of the seesaw move up and down because the seesaw is another type of **LEVER**—one that has a fulcrum in the middle.

When the weight on both sides of the **LEVER** is the same, the lever stays level, or is balanced. When more weight is put on one side, that side goes down and the other side goes up. A balance scale is an another example of this type of lever.

On my way back inside, I meet Ms. Jacqueline. She's moving into our building today. She has a lot of boxes to move! Ms. Jacqueline moves her boxes off of the moving truck by walking them down the ramp. If she couldn't use the ramp to unload her boxes, she would have to climb in and out of the truck with every box. That would take a long time!

inclined plane

A ramp is a type of simple machine called an **INCLINED PLANE**. An inclined plane is a flat surface that is higher on one end. There are different types of inclined planes. Ramps, ladders, and playground slides are all examples of inclined planes.

Mr. Perron is the handyman in our building. He stops by to fix the knob on our door. I ask if I can help, too. Mr. Perron uses a screwdriver to put a new doorknob on our door and uses **SCREWS** to hold it in place.

A **SCREW** is a type of simple machine that is used to hold things together. Screws have threads around them that keep them securely in place.

The top of a **SCREW** is called the head. A screwdriver fits perfectly into the notch on the head of a screw so you can turn it and tighten it into place.

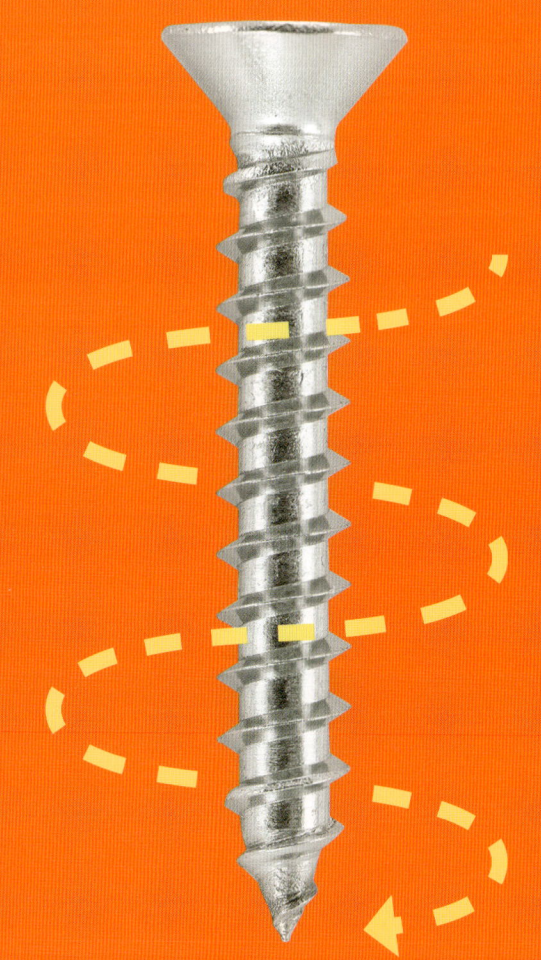

screw

That evening, I notice that my lamp needs a new lightbulb. I ask my dad to replace the light bulb for me. My dad takes out the old light bulb and screws in a new one. Now we have enough light to read my bedtime stories!

screw

A light bulb has a **SCREW** on one end that holds it in place. Instead of using a screwdriver, this type of screw is screwed in by turning it with your hand. Bottle tops, jar lids, and toothpaste caps are examples of screws.

It's fun to live in my building!

I get to see my neighbors every day. They do lots of interesting things, and sometimes I get to help!